MW00852674

MEETINGS THAT GET RESULTS

MEETINGS THAT GET RESULTS

BRIAN TRACY

AMACOM AMERICAN MANAGEMENT ASSOCIATION
New York · Atlanta · Brussels · Chicago · Mexico City
San Francisco · Shanghai · Tokyo · Toronto · Washington, D.C.

This publication is designed to provide accurate and authoritative information in regard to the subject matter covered. It is sold with the understanding that the publisher is not engaged in rendering legal, accounting, or other professional service. If legal advice or other expert assistance is required, the services of a competent professional person should be sought.

Library of Congress Cataloging-in-Publication Data

Names: Tracy, Brian, author.
Title: Meetings that get results / Brian Tracy.
Description: New York : American Management Association, [2016] | Includes index.
Identifiers: LCCN 2015038240 | ISBN 9780814437056 (hardcover) | ISBN 9780814437063 (ebook)
Subjects: LCSH: Business meetings. | Meetings.
Classification: LCC HF5734.5.T73 2016 | DDC 658.4/56—dc23 LC record available at http://lccn.loc.gov/2015038240

About AMA

American Management Association (www.amanet.org) is a world leader in talent development, advancing the skills of individuals to drive business success. Our mission is to support the goals of individuals and organizations through a complete range of products and services, including classroom and virtual seminars, webcasts, webinars, podcasts, conferences, corporate and government solutions, business books, and research. AMA's approach to improving performance combines experiential learning—learning through doing—with opportunities for ongoing professional growth at every step of one's career journey.

Printing number
10 9 8 7 6 5 4 3 2 1

CONTENTS

Introduction

MEETINGS ARE an essential part of the life of every organization. As a manager, one-quarter or more of your career will be spent in group meetings. As much as 70 percent to 80 percent of your career is going to be spent face-to-face and one-on-one with other people as well as in groups.

The more people there are in your workplace and the greater the complexity required for the performance of interrelated tasks, the more necessary it is for people to meet in groups to solve problems, make decisions, share information, and exchange views and opinions.

My favorite expression is that "meetings are management in action." They are a major opportunity for you to display managerial competence (or lack thereof) as well as to develop your communication skills, to influence and persuade others, and to advance the goals of the organization.

However, meetings are like advertising. It is estimated that 50 percent of the dollars spent on advertising are wasted, but nobody knows which 50 percent it is. It is also estimated that half of the time spent in meetings is wasted, but nobody knows how to eliminate the unnecessary half.

Many meetings go on too long, are ineffective, are not results-oriented, or are vague and directionless. Nonetheless, they cannot be avoided. Meetings remain absolutely essential in the business environment and essential to your success.

Influence Others

In this book, you will learn how to manage and participate in meetings more effectively so that you get the maximum return on the time invested in meeting with other people.

As a manager, the way you plan and conduct a meeting and the way you perform in a meeting are major factors in your career success. In a meeting, you are being observed by both your supervisors and your subordinates. Your superiors especially will be very alert to the quality and quantity of contribution you make in a meeting. If you handle yourself well in meetings, you'll be hallmarked as an up-and-coming leader. You can shine and be a star contributor, or you can bomb. It's up to you, but you cannot hide.

If you are the leader, your subordinates will evaluate your credibility, competence, intelligence, and your general personality by the way you conduct meetings.

Successful executives are those who know how to run meetings well and perform effectively in a meeting environment.

Peter Drucker said that "meetings are the primary tool of management." Since a major part of your career will be spent in meetings, it is essential for your success that you learn how to get the very most out of meetings and how to ensure that the meetings in which you participate achieve the results desired.

Save Time

If you become excellent in participating in and conducting meetings, you can add as much as 40 percent of lost time back into your day for doing productive work and getting more results, which will help you move rapidly up the corporate ladder. But if you cannot function excellently in meetings, you cannot be successful in management.

In this book, we are going to talk about two main types of meetings. The first one, with which you are most familiar, is the group meeting where people come together for a variety of reasons. The second is the one-on-one meeting, where you meet with one or a small number of people to negotiate, interview, discipline, hire, fire, reward, delegate, or carry out other managerial activities.

This book includes twenty-one key ideas derived from many years of study and research into the organization and coordination of effective meetings. When you begin incorporating these ideas, or even some of them, into your meeting management strategy, you will become so much more effective in meetings, and probably quite quickly, that you will not believe the difference.

ONE

Types of Meetings

THOMAS J. WATSON, the founder of IBM, said that the starting point in making meetings more effective is to think carefully about the meeting in advance.

Determine what kind of meeting is being held and then structure the meeting in such a way that you maximize the time of the participants. Too many meetings are held spontaneously and ad hoc, with no real thought, particular preparation, purpose, or clear goal in mind.

There are five different types of meetings. Some of them overlap, but each meeting type has its own requirements.

Information Sharing
The first is an information-sharing meeting. This is when you bring people together to review progress and to share

information in a roundtable way. The participants' role is to bring others up-to-date on their activities. A typical staff meeting is a good example.

This is a process-oriented meeting. It is not aimed at a specific target or goal but is part of an ongoing process and is a very important means of communication. Most executives polled estimate that information-sharing meetings are the second most important form of communication in an organization. (The most important form is the one-on-one meeting.)

Problem Solving

The second type of meeting is for problem solving. These meetings are goal- and mission-oriented. The purpose of the meeting is to find a solution to a specific problem. These meetings take place frequently, usually ad hoc, and are put together quickly. Problem-solving meetings vary in length depending on the size and complexity of the problem to be solved.

Operational

The third type of meeting is an operational meeting when you bring together people from different departments. The purpose of this kind of meeting is to acquaint representatives of different departments of a company with "the big picture."

Committee

The fourth type of meeting is the committee meeting. This is a regularly scheduled meeting with a standard format and agenda, and with the same group of people who come together to monitor and review progress, plan ongoing activities, and give and receive feedback.

A good example of the committee meeting is the quality circle or quality team meeting. This is where a committee of employees gets together on a regular basis to review past efforts, talk about what they can do to improve quality, and develop recommendations for management.

Teaching and Training

The fifth type of meeting is the teaching and training or seminar meeting. The purpose here is to instruct the participants in some new subject. An example would be when new equipment or technology is being introduced, or when you are initiating a new program.

Many meetings have elements of all five types. But to make a meeting effective, it must be clear to everyone which basic type of meeting is being held.

TWO

Define the Purpose of the Meeting

THE STARTING point of meeting effectiveness is clarity of purpose. What is the reason for the meeting in the first place? Think it through in advance and ask why the meeting is being held at all. Guard against the tendency of slipping into the habit of holding meetings just for the sake of them.

Questions to Ask

There are some questions that you can ask to clarify the purpose of the meeting.

First, is the meeting necessary? Is there some other way that you can accomplish the objective? Is there another way to hold this meeting or to solve this problem? If your purpose is information sharing, can you pass information on by phone, e-mail, or through a website?

Remember, if it is not necessary to meet, it is necessary *not* to meet—because the meeting ends up being a major time waster. Whenever time is wasted, morale and performance suffer.

What would be the worst possible outcome if no meeting were held at all? If you find that nothing much would happen, or that business could be taken care of in other ways, then you should discipline yourself to not hold the meeting.

Second, who must attend the meeting? Who is absolutely essential to this meeting and, of course, who is not essential and should not be there? It is a big mistake to invite people who do not need to be at the meeting because they won't be able to contribute or take away any value.

Crystallize the Reason

Third, what is the purpose of the meeting? The measure of clarity of purpose is that you can define on paper the purpose of the meeting in twenty-five words or less. If you are unable to do this, it could very well be that you don't really know what the purpose is yourself.

Ask yourself the question, "If this meeting worked out perfectly, what would be the result? What would happen? What would people do afterward?"

When you are crystal clear about the goals and objectives for the meeting, when you can define the purpose of the meeting and why you are holding it, it becomes much easier for you to plan the meeting, the agenda, and the particulars that you want to cover.

Trying to Solve the Wrong Problem

In some cases, even when you have defined the goals and objectives for the meeting, you discover later that the meeting did not yield effective results. One reason is that you may have misidentified a problem that you wanted to resolve.

For example, in our sales consulting work, the purpose of many meetings is to resolve a familiar problem: Our sales are too low.

We will ask, "What else is the problem?"

The answer may be, "We are not attracting enough new customers."

If this is the correct answer, the solution would be to change or improve the advertising and promotional activities to increase customer acquisition.

We then ask, "What else is the problem?"

The next answer may be that "our competitors' sales are too high in comparison with ours."

If this is the true definition of the problem, the solution may be to change our product offerings, offer products or services that are new or different, aim our sales efforts at different customers, lower our prices, or offer something new and different that sets us apart from our competitors.

Our meetings are successful because we drill down to the real problems that need to be resolved, not the surface problems that are easy to see.

Meetings as Company Investments

THERE ARE costs associated with each meeting, both direct and indirect. As a business, there must be an expected return on investment of those costs, and the return should be substantially greater than the amount that the company is paying to hold the meeting in the first place.

If someone came to you and asked for an authorization to spend several hundred dollars on a piece of machinery or a project, you would want to know exactly what value you would receive and how the company would benefit.

The Cost of Meetings

When you convene a meeting, you have to recognize that the cost of the people in that meeting can be enormous. A simple way to determine the cost is to multiply the hourly income of the participants by the number of hours of the meeting. If these people are earning $50,000 to $100,000 per year, that works out to $25 to $50 per hour for each participant. If you invite ten of these highly paid people to a meeting, it can cost the company up to $500, or more, for a single hour. Imagine paying that to each person out of your own pocket.

Continually ask yourself if the expense of this meeting is justified. What will be the return on investment if the meeting is successful and productive? Is it worth spending this money? If you are taking people away from other productive work, the meeting has to be more productive and valuable than the activities they would otherwise be accomplishing.

Ensure Maximum ROI

Identify the things that you can do before and during the meeting to make sure that the return on investment is at its maximum. Your job as the meeting planner and organizer is to increase the value of the meeting so that when people adjourn they say, "That was a really good meeting. This was a valuable use of time."

One of my favorite time management laws is called the Law of the Excluded Alternative. It simply says that choosing *to do* one thing means simultaneously choosing *not to do* all other things you could be doing at the same time.

Since you can only do one thing at a time, whenever you choose something to do, such as participating in a meeting, you are choosing not to do everything and anything else that may be of greater value. What you are seeking is the highest ROTI—*return on time invested.* Think about your time, and the time of every other person, as if you were paying people in cash at their hourly rate for the time that they spend in the meeting.

FOUR

Determine the Agenda

THIS IS THE starting point of holding effective meetings. Always prepare a written agenda and provide a copy for each participant. One of the biggest mistakes in any meeting, formal or informal, no matter how short, is to start off without an agenda.

When I was younger, I would meet with my boss on a regular basis, usually daily. But I found that if we were not very careful, we could talk for as long as an hour and not have reached closure on anything. This state of affairs was dissatisfying to both of us.

Without any training or preparation, one day I wrote out a list of the things that I wanted to discuss with him and brought an extra photocopy of my handwritten list to the meeting. As soon as I showed my boss the list, he brightened up.

Increase Effectiveness

In no time at all, we were able to go down the list, discuss each point, and reach a decision on what was going to be done or not done. We quite quickly cut our meeting time from sixty to twenty minutes, and we got much more accomplished.

From then on, my boss was always open to meeting with me because he knew that our time together would be highly productive. As a result, I was given more and more responsibilities and eventually was moved onto the fast track in my company.

Write It Down

Always start with a written agenda, even if you just put it together a couple of minutes before the event.

The agenda should begin with a one-sentence description of the purpose or objective of the meeting. If you cannot boil it down to a single sentence, it probably means that the purpose of the meeting is too vague. It is going to be an ineffective meeting and a waste of time for most, if not all, of the participants.

But when you write out the agenda—starting with a purpose statement—it forces you to think through what you are doing and why you are doing it. It gives you greater clarity regarding how each of the items on the agenda can be best dealt with.

Organize the Agenda

Organize the topics in order of importance, by priority. Ask yourself, "If we were interrupted after we had only discussed one thing on this list, what one item would be the most important?"

By starting with the most important items, you are ensuring that they will be covered and the least important items will be set aside for another day if the meeting is forced to end before you get through the entire agenda.

When possible, distribute the agenda twenty-four to forty-eight hours in advance, either by hard copy or by e-mail. This allows people to prepare and to think through the issues. They can come to the meeting ready to make a valuable contribution that, in turn, increases your return on investment of time. The more important the meeting, the more important the agenda and its advance distribution.

Who Should Attend?

Restrict attendance to the minimum number of essential people. When I was a young executive, I felt that it was only fair to invite everybody to the regular staff meetings so that all could participate and feel they were a part of the team. What I found after a while was that a lot of them didn't really want to come to the meeting, and that my exercise in democracy was an exercise in frustration.

From then on, I restricted attendance to only those people who were necessary to deal with the items on the agenda. Everyone else was free to participate or not participate.

Ask yourself: Who really needs to be at this meeting? Who can contribute and needs to participate in the decision making or problem solving? Who requires this information, and is there a better way to get it to them?

FIVE

How to Run a Meeting

YOUR ABILITY to lead a meeting is a critical part of your success in management. This skill is one of the marks of leadership that is most evident to people in your organization. As Peter Drucker wrote, "The key tools of the executive are the meeting, the presentation, and the report." You must be excellent at all three.

Clarity Is Essential

Perhaps the most important word in success is the word *clarity*. Fully 95 percent of your success will be determined by your being absolutely clear about what it is you want to accomplish and how you are going to accomplish it.

Perhaps 95 percent of your problems will come from a lack of clarity as well. This is why it is so important for you to begin with a clear, written outline of the purpose of the meeting, even if it is only one sentence. When everyone sits down, you can open a meeting by saying, "We are holding this meeting today for this reason and to accomplish these goals and objectives."

Plan the Opening

The first five to seven minutes of any meeting are the most important part of that meeting. The opening sets the foundation, establishes the parameters, organizes the terms of reference, and tells everyone in the room why they are there, for how long, and what they need to accomplish.

You may even consider writing out your introduction, word for word, and then reading it at the beginning of the meeting. This clarity will allow a person who doesn't know you or the situation to get up to speed right at the start.

Be specific and punctual with regard to the timing. Everyone should know exactly when the meeting starts and stops. This information should be printed at the top of your agenda, but you will want to restate it in your introduction.

Start on Time

Begin right on time. Do not penalize the people who were there on time by waiting for others who are late. Assume that the latecomer is not coming at all and begin the meeting immediately. This piece of advice was invaluable to me when I was coming up as a manager.

If someone comes in late and discovers that they have missed important information, refuse to start over or to review it for them. By catering to the latecomers, you are actually punishing the people who are punctual. When the latecomer looks a bit incompetent, he will eventually get the message and be more punctual next time.

Many companies have a policy where if a meeting is called for 10:00 am, they lock the doors from the inside at 10:01. You only have to do that once to get people to be on time in the future.

Make a Statement

If the purpose of a meeting is to solve a problem, you say: "We are here to discuss this problem and to come to a decision, conclusion, or resolution on moving forward. Here are the facts of the problem. Here is the information that we have, the alternatives that we have considered, and our market intelligence. Now, what do we do from here?"

Encourage open discussion. It is important that you invite input from each person, not only the people who have a lot to contribute and are eager to talk, but also from those who are more self-contained and less likely to speak up. Especially, you want input from those people who may be a bit reluctant to try to compete with more aggressive or assertive people. Quiet people often have a lot to contribute, if encouraged and given the chance.

The way I get people to open up in a discussion is to use the "round-robin method." As the group leader, you start off the meeting and go right around the table, inviting each person to speak, in turn. As the meeting leader, you speak and contribute last, not first. When it is your turn, you can comment on what the others have said, state your opinion, and if necessary, go around the room again.

This is very much like starting an engine. Once you have gone around the table once or twice, everyone will be speaking up and making a contribution.

Refuse to Dominate

The best meeting leaders do not dominate the meeting. They encourage others to talk. The natural tendency of meeting leaders, unfortunately, is to speak as much as 50 percent of the time, on average. The more they speak, the quieter and less involved the other people in the meeting become. Once the leader has dominated the conversation for any period of time, most people lose interest in the subject and look forward to getting back to work.

Instead, as the group leader you should be a *facilitator*. Avoid lecturing or hogging the discussion. If you fail to invite everyone to contribute, you will naturally tend to speak more and more just because you are the one in charge.

Stay on Track

Keep the discussion on track. A key job of the meeting leader is to keep bringing people back to the main issue. Stick to the items on the agenda and don't allow discussion to stray or wander.

Press for closure. Once you start talking on a subject, discuss it thoroughly but press for closure on what has been decided and who is going to do what, and by when, before you move on to the next item on the agenda.

The inability to keep on track and to press for closure are two major time wasters—and the major complaints from people who attend meetings.

Summarize at the end of each discussion point and at the end of the meeting. Set out and restate your time and action schedules, your implementation plans, and your assignments. Then have everyone in the meeting agree on what has been decided, and who is going to do what.

Finally, distribute the minutes of the meeting within twenty-four hours. The more important the decisions that have been taken, the more important it is that you have them distributed in writing so that if anyone has questions, they can get back to you immediately. If there are no questions, then everyone accepts the record of the meeting as you sent it to them.

SIX

Participating in Meetings

HOW YOU participate in a meeting is carefully observed by everyone in attendance—your superiors and subordinates alike. You are either a participator or a combination of a leader and participator in a meeting. In either case, you have a specific and important role. As a leader you are in the spotlight, but even as a participant you are still being watched all the time.

In observing, conducting, and participating in thousands of meetings over the years, I have witnessed executives who have moved their careers from the slow track to the fast track with the quality of their involvement and engagement in a meeting with their superiors.

Fast-Track Your Career

In one experience, I conducted a three-day strategic planning meeting for the senior executives of a billion-dollar company with branches all over the country. Many of the executives had been with the company for two or three decades. They took their jobs for granted. They did not prepare, and it was clear that they had not read and reviewed their work in advance of the meeting.

When we went around the table and asked for questions and contributions, they acted as if this sort of thing was a bit beneath their dignity. Meanwhile, there were two executives from operating branches of this organization located more than 1,000 miles from head office.

These two managers, however, were extremely well prepared. They had done their homework. They had comments, observations, and suggestions on every point, for the entire three days. It was clear to everyone in the room that these men were smart, knowledgeable, and took their responsibilities seriously.

People Are Watching

After each session, I would walk in the hotel gardens with the president of the company, commenting and discussing what was going on in the meeting and the contributions that each of the executives was making. The president was disappointed, although not surprised, with the poor participation of the more senior executives. But at the same time, he was amazed and delighted with the energy and intelligence of the two younger managers.

Two weeks after this strategic planning session, which clarified the values, goals, and plans for the future of the company, the photos and biographies of those two executives appeared in the national newspapers with the announcements that they had both been promoted to vice presidential positions in this company. They advanced their careers by as much as five or ten years because of their participation in this meeting.

Not long after, the "retirement" of several of the older executives was also announced, which came as no surprise to the people at the meeting.

Do Your Homework

The key to effective participation in meetings, as in every other area, is detailed preparation in anticipation of the meeting. Do your research and your homework. Make it obvious to others that you are ready for this meeting—perhaps more ready than anyone else. Preparation is the mark of the professional.

The person chairing the meeting, who is often someone who can have a great influence on your future, really appreciates it when you come prepared to deal intelligently with the agenda items. On the other hand, if you have not done your homework, it is immediately obvious to everyone. This unpreparedness is often felt as an insult to the meeting planner and the meeting leader.

Speak Up Early

The first five minutes are critical. People who get involved in the meeting within the first five minutes seem to have the greatest influence on the outcome of the meeting. The best way to establish that you are a valuable member of the group is not by making comments or statements, but by asking intelligent questions of the meeting leader or the other people who are reporting in their areas of activity.

If you wait for fifteen or twenty minutes to speak up or to get involved, your influence on the rest of the meeting drops by half. If you only get involved in the last part of a meeting, you will have almost no influence on what is decided, except to the degree to which you have power and authority within the corporate hierarchy. People will simply ignore you.

In the first five minutes, you should ask a question, make a positive statement, or support what someone else is saying.

Have Something to Contribute

When I conduct staff meetings and some of the group members sit there silently, contributing little, I point out to them an important fact: "Those who do not contribute to a meeting are considered to be people who have nothing to contribute. Those who do not say anything at a meeting are considered to be those who have nothing of value to say."

Whenever I point this out to the quiet members of the group, they immediately arouse themselves and begin commenting or asking questions. No one wants to be seen as a useless or irrelevant person in front of their peers.

Be an active participant. Be a player. Use body language. Lean forward, smile, nod, and encourage others when they are speaking. Pay close attention to the person who is speaking, take notes, and make eye contact. Make it clear that this meeting is really important to you. When you do, you compliment the meeting leader, identify yourself as a person of importance, and contribute value to the other attendees.

Potential leaders are often identified by the way they perform in meetings. Sometimes your performance in a meeting will bring you to the attention of a key person and open up new opportunities for added responsibilities and assignments.

SEVEN

Problem-Solving Meetings

THE MOST common and often the most important type of meeting is the problem-solving meeting. There are ways to hold these meetings so that they work well, but most problem-solving meetings wander around in circles. People forget that the purpose is to define the problem clearly, find a solution that everyone agrees with, and then to take action.

Here are some ideas for a successful problem-solving meeting.

Define the Problem Clearly

It is amazing how often it is that each person in the meeting has a different definition of the problem under discussion. This wastes an enormous amount of time.

Instead, ask, "What exactly is the problem?" Words are important. Clearly define the problem in writing, on paper, or even better, on a flipchart or whiteboard so that everyone can see it and read it clearly.

In medicine, it is said that "accurate diagnosis is half the cure." It is the same in solving a problem. Accurately diagnosing the problem in the first place can save you 50 percent or more of the time and cost of solving the problem later on.

What Else Is the Problem?

Once you have agreed on a definition, you then ask, "What else is the problem?" Beware of a problem for which there is only one definition. Have we determined the correct problem? Is it really a problem, or is it an opportunity? The more definitions of the problem that you can generate, the more likely it is that you will generate the right definition, which often leads to an obvious and workable solution.

There is the story of the man who "jumped on his horse and rode off in all directions." This is often an accurate description of a problem-solving meeting where everyone quickly concludes that the first definition of a problem is the correct one. The very worst thing you can do is to ride off in all directions to solve the wrong problem.

Keep Asking

Again and again, we ask the question, "What else is the problem?" You will be amazed at the number of different answers you can generate with this method. This technique is used today at the highest levels of discussion, debate, and problem solving in small and large organizations worldwide.

Once everyone has agreed on a single best definition of the real problem with which you are wrestling, you then ask, "What is the solution?" Sometimes the solution will be simple, clear, and obvious. But whatever the first answer, it is merely a working hypothesis. It is the starting point of developing the correct solution, not the end point.

Beware of a problem for which there is only one solution. Ask the magic question: What else is the solution?

Four Ways to Change

We have found over time that there are only four ways to solve a problem or change a situation:

One: You can do *more* of certain things. And what should you do more of? You should do more of those things that are working for you and achieving the best and most cost-effective results.

Two: You can do *less* of other things. And what should you be doing less of? You should be doing less of those things that are not getting you the kind of results that you desire.

Three: You can *start doing* something completely new or different. You can offer new products or services. You can offer new prices or processes. You can use new sales and marketing methods. You can develop new distribution channels or move into different markets.

Starting something new or different is the hardest thing of all. As Machiavelli said, "There is nothing more difficult or dangerous than the initiation of a new order of things. It will be resisted by everyone whose interests are threatened, and only weakly supported by those who might most benefit."

But it is in starting something new that the major changes and breakthroughs take place in both personal and business life. What should you start doing that you are not doing today?

Four: You can *stop* doing certain things altogether. Whenever you are wrestling with a problem or difficulty, ask yourself, "Is there anything that we are doing today that, knowing what we now know, we wouldn't start up again today if we had to do it over?"

Develop Decision Criteria

That is, determine the boundary conditions for the solution. In other words, what does the decision have to accomplish? How much money can be spent? How many people will you require? How much time will it take? When does this problem need to be solved by? Take the time to make these determinations and then compare each possible solution against them.

Quantity Determines Quality

The rule regarding solutions is to aim for quantity versus quality. This is known as the "divergent thinking phase," where you examine as many alternatives as possible. Avoid the tendency to suggest only one or two ideas and then settle on one. Keep asking, "What else is the solution?"

There seems to be a direct relationship between the quantity of solutions generated and the quality of the solution that you eventually settle on. The more conflict, argument, and disagreement there is in the meeting over what the solution might be, the more likely it is that you will emerge with a higher-quality solution. The less conflict there is, the more likely it is that you will get groupthink, a consensual solution that, in many cases, will be a poor one.

Test Your Decision

Once you have settled on a solution, test it against the boundary conditions that you have discussed. What are your limits and parameters? Which of your solutions fit the decision criteria the best? In this way, you focus on the issues rather than on the people involved. You focus on solutions rather than personalities.

After thorough discussion, you then make the very best decision you possibly can, rather than no decision at all. Make sure that your solution is clear and measurable and that everyone agrees with it. Avoid generalizations.

Once you have defined the problem clearly and settled on the very best decision, all things considered, you must then decide who is going to implement your solution. Assign specific people to carry out all or parts of the solution.

You then set specific deadlines for completion of the agreed-on tasks.

Measure and Monitor

It is important to agree on how the implementation of the decision is to be monitored and controlled. You have probably had the experience where everyone gets together for a problem-solving meeting and, after considerable discussion, solutions are agreed on and the meeting breaks up.

Then, a couple of weeks later, you all come back together again and nothing has happened. Why?

Usually it is because of the four people involved in every group activity: "everybody, somebody, anybody, and nobody."

"Everybody" agrees on the problem, the solution, the plan of action, and what is to be done. However, you fail to determine the actual "somebody" who is going to be responsible for carrying out the solution. As a result, people conclude that "anybody" can and should do the job, so there is nothing to worry about. But at the end of the day, it turns out that "nobody" has actually taken action and done the job that was agreed on.

EIGHT

The Decision-Making Model for Meetings

PERHAPS THE most important goal that you can achieve in problem-solving meetings is a full consensus by all of the participants. Without full consensus, there will be a natural tendency for people to withhold their support for the decision and actively sabotage the decision because they do not agree with it.

There are three levels in the process of developing consensus.

Encourage Openness

The first level is open discussion. When you go through the problem-solving process, as discussed in Chapter 7, you invite input and ideas from everyone. Each person is required and encouraged to contribute input to the discussion.

It is the same in meetings. Open discussion is important because without it, if someone disagrees or objects to the decision, they will withhold their support and just appear as if they are going along with the group.

The best way to get everyone singing from the same page is by encouraging people to openly challenge and disagree with anyone else. Sometimes this process becomes quite heated. People dig in their heels and become adamant about their point of view, even if others disagree. This is a normal and natural part of the process. Your job as the meeting leader is to allow and encourage this process to continue for as long as it takes.

In most cases, the most amazing thing happens. If people are allowed to fully express themselves, whether or not others agree with them, or whether or not their point of view is accepted, they become much more supportive of whatever decision the group ultimately takes.

Listen Patiently to Everyone

Not long ago, we were brought in by the president of a national organization to conduct a two-day strategic planning program. There was one major change that the organization had to make to survive and to adjust to the dramatic changes taking place in the industry. But one of the senior executives was adamantly opposed to any change in this area. He wielded a lot of power and could have been a fatal obstacle to the success of this process.

As the meeting leader, I encouraged him to express his opinions, which he did quite vocally, speaking loudly and dominating the meeting. At the end of the first day, the president of the organization took me aside and confessed that she did not think this process was going to be successful. There was simply too much resistance and negativity on the part of this key person. But I told her not to worry.

Prepare to Be Surprised

The next day, we continued the meeting where we had left off. I once again reminded everyone that there seemed to be general agreement that we take this new course of action—a course of action to which this executive was vigorously opposed. To the surprise of everyone, he announced that he had thought over his position during the night and had come to the conclusion that his ideas were no longer consistent with the new situation. He changed his mind 100 percent and announced that he completely supported the new direction.

Clear Decision

The second part of the consensual decision-making model is to arrive at a clear decision. But this is not a democratic decision; it is a *consensual* decision.

This means that there are no factions within the group who disagree with the decision. You take the time to discuss the various possibilities and alternative courses of action that are available until you reach a point where everyone agrees 100 percent. There is no dissent. Everyone is satisfied with the agreed-on decision.

This process often requires a good deal of patience on the part of the meeting leader. You need to be calm and positive. In my experience, the point of consensus is often not reached until near the end of what might have been a highly contentious meeting.

Keep asking questions and eliciting the thinking and opinions of each person. Continue going around the table and inviting people to comment. Let the process unfold at its own time, knowing that if you remain calm and positive, at a certain point, something happens. Everyone seems to agree with everyone else. There is no further argument or dissent. The discussion almost naturally comes to a close.

Get a Full Commitment

The third part of the consensual model is *full commitment.* This does not mean that people no longer have problems or concerns. It simply means that, despite uncertainties and misgivings, everyone commits 100 percent to making the decision successful. No one withholds support. Everyone is "on board."

Someone Must Make the Final Decision

Everyone knows or has heard about the decisive meeting prior to the D-day invasion of France on June 6, 1944. Senior military leaders planned for this invasion for more than two years. More than 3 million men were organized and camped all over England in preparation for the big day.

Everything depended on the weather. The invasion was actually scheduled for June 5, but on that day, a storm came up in the English Channel that would make the crossing of hundreds of ships far too dangerous and even impossible to pull off.

That night, the weather forecasters came to the senior military leaders gathered with General Dwight D. Eisenhower and said that there would be a pause in the bad weather on June 6. A window of opportunity would open up but could quickly close if the weather changed.

After considering all of the information and looking into the faces of all the other generals around the table, with everyone waiting expectantly, Eisenhower finally said, "Let's go!"

From that moment of decision, there was no hesitation on the part of anyone. There was 100 percent commitment. No one held back. The Normandy invasion was launched, and, as we know, was successful. It was one of the greatest consensus decisions in history.

Even when others don't entirely agree with the decision, the results are much better if you have gone through a detailed process of discussion, made a clear decision, and then requested full commitment and support. This is a true mark of leadership.

NINE

Problems in Meetings

THERE ARE several reasons why problem-solving meetings are often counterproductive and frustrating. Be alert to some of the weaknesses and avoid them if you want important meetings to be effective.

Some experts say all meetings are basically problem-solving meetings. All meetings are held to determine a course of action, resolve a problem or difficulty, or find a solution. If this is the case, then 50 percent to 60 percent of your time every day is spent in this type of meeting. It is important that you be aware of the obstacles to effective thinking and good decision making.

Groupthink

The first challenge in meetings is groupthink. This occurs when the group has a tendency to move quickly to a conclusion without considering enough different ways of defining the problem or the solution. Rather than weighing and measuring different decisions against each other, the group moves like a "herd" and settles on a single decision early in the discussion. Sometimes this is called *convergent thinking*, where the group moves to a particular solution without considering a greater variety of alternatives.

Alfred P. Sloan, the founder of General Motors, was aware of this danger. When he called a meeting to discuss and agree on a course of action, and when everyone seemed to be in agreement with the solution, he would bring the meeting to an end and table the discussion.

Then he would tell the assembled executives that if everyone was in agreement early in the discussion, it probably meant that no one had really given very much thought to the issue under consideration. He would instruct everyone to go away and think about the situation and come back with questions and disagreements. He insisted that people take the issues more seriously. He had found, with experience, that problems resolved by groupthink were solutions that were invariably worse than those that had been carefully considered.

A complex problem and its solution need to be argued over and dissected for the pros and cons of the issue. If the solution arises too early and too easily, and everyone goes along with it, it is probably wrong. It needs to be thought through at greater depth.

Let's All Get Along

Another weakness that emerges in problem-solving or decision-making meetings is the desire to avoid conflict and to say, "Let's not argue or fight."

People think that if they want to get along, they have to go along. The people at the meeting become more concerned with getting along with each other and being friends than they are with challenging each other and expressing disagreement. Conflict avoidance takes priority over solution quality, which almost always generates suboptimal solutions.

Often, the group feels that any solution will do. It is late in the day or late in the week, and the members of the decision-making group want to come to a resolution and move on as soon as possible. The group values "getting any decision" more highly than getting a good decision. The group wants closure so that they can get on to something else. They don't want to make the effort to think through the hard issues to come up with a superior solution.

Louder and Faster

Another problem in decision-making meetings is that there is a tendency for the group to be more influenced by those who speak out more, louder or faster. An authoritative, dominant, or Type A personality will usually speak more fluently and articulately, with more command of information and more conviction than others. This type of person may unduly sway the other members of the group.

For this reason the manager or group leader should be like an *orchestra conductor*, guiding and directing others rather than dominating the meeting. A good position for you to take at the beginning is to have no fixed opinion on the matter under discussion; instead, you are going to leave it to the members of the group to thrash it out until they come to a consensus.

Anyone who speaks louder, faster, or with greater self-confidence will have greater influence on the other people in the meeting. This is a common technique that some people use to impose their personality and ideas on others. The danger is that if the people who speak the loudest have the greatest influence, they can cause the group to move toward or settle on a poor decision or one that is not the best decision for this issue.

Take Charge

As the group leader, there are two strategies you can use. First, take the loud-talking person aside before the meeting and ask him to give others an opportunity to speak. Second, when someone begins to dominate the meeting by speaking louder and faster, you can say something like, "That is a good idea. Let's hear what some of the others have to say about this." Encourage other people to contribute their best thinking and block for them so that they get a chance to speak.

Politics in Decision Making

A major factor in ineffective decision making, and a problem in meetings, is politics. Someone has power and authority and intimidates others in the meeting; meanwhile, everyone else wants to be seen as a team player, so they go along with the person in the meeting who has the most authority.

Because of this political discomfort, people can find themselves agreeing with things they are not really comfortable with. Political decisions often bring about the worst possible decisions for the organization.

The solutions to these general problems are always the same. Have a written agenda. Give everyone a chance to talk. Encourage the quieter people to fully express themselves and run interference for them by not allowing interruptions when someone is speaking. Remember, the meeting is one of the most important tools of the manager. Your ability to conduct excellent meetings—meetings that get results—is indispensable to your future.

TEN

Reasons for Ineffective Meetings

A MAJOR reason for ineffective meetings is *vague goals*. People are not sure why the meeting is being held and what the goal of the meeting is supposed to be. There is either no written agenda or the items on the agenda are not clear. This is why you should announce at the beginning of the meeting the purpose of the meeting and what you hope to accomplish.

Poor Meeting Leadership

Another major reason for ineffective meetings is the conduct of the leader. Meeting leaders can make a number of key mistakes that will destroy the potential of any meeting. These mistakes include:

▪ **Starting the meeting late.** Some leaders hold off starting the meeting on time to allow latecomers a chance to arrive. What happens is that the people who are on time must wait at every meeting. Eventually, they decide that they are wasting their time and start arriving late at the meetings. Soon a standing 10:00 a.m. meeting never gets started till 10:30 a.m. Decide when the meeting is supposed to start and don't deviate.

▪ **Losing control of the meeting.** Sometimes the leader is succinct, but other participants are long-winded and go off on a tangent. Ineffective meetings result when the leader fails to keep the group on track and allows the conversation to wander off topic. Many people love to talk and hear the sound of their own voice. They continually jump to subjects that are of interest to them, even though they have no relevance to the meeting. In other cases, everyone around the table gets involved in a heated discussion that goes in circles, with no resolution in sight. A leader must always keep the meeting on track and moving forward.

▪ **Dominating the discussion.** A meeting is not a speech. If a leader is doing most of the talking, then the meeting is useless.

▪ **Failing to reach a conclusion.** Some meetings are ineffective because the group fails to push through to a conclusion. They go back and forth in the discussion but are unwilling to take a stake and agree on a final answer. They may be afraid to be wrong. They may fear that they do not have enough information to make a good decision, or that it will be held against them if the decision does not work. Meeting leaders must have the courage to push for a solution.

Lack of Group Participation

As stated above a meeting is useless if the other participants don't feel encouraged to join in. One way that you can avoid dominating the meeting and suppressing the comments and ideas of the other participants is to delegate meeting leadership. Whenever possible, assign the chairing of the meeting to someone else. This is a wonderful way to build the skills and confidence of your subordinates.

Meeting leadership is a wonderful training tool that gives employees the opportunity to organize their thoughts and perform in front of a group of their peers. In my experience, when you delegate meeting leadership to staff members, even those in junior positions, they tend to take it quite seriously. They put a good deal of effort into planning the meeting and preparing the agenda. By delegating the responsibility of conducting the meeting, you can save yourself a lot of time and effort.

Very often, in my management meetings, I assign a different staff member the job of chairing the meeting each time. Without exception, I have been delighted with the results. Even shy people who don't speak up very much turn out to be excellent leaders when they are put in charge of a meeting.

Lack of Follow-Up

Sometimes meetings lead to some great ideas, but those ideas go nowhere. That is because the leader did not put in place the next steps—namely, who is going to do what. The purpose of a meeting is not to talk; the purpose of a meeting is to prepare for action. It's the responsibility of the leader to make sure that action is taken. Specific performance measures must be put on the decision that emerges from the meeting, and there must be a deadline for completion.

My favorite question is always, "What is our next action?" What do we do now, and who is going to do it? When is it going to be done, and how are we going to measure it?

The greater clarity and focus you have, and the more you bring each discussion point to a clear conclusion, the more productive and valuable the meeting will be. People will look forward to subsequent meetings with you, and your star will continue to rise.

Don't Forget the Venue!

Imagine conducting a meeting with a rock band practicing next door (it actually happened to me once). Poor sound, missing equipment, a room that is too cold or too hot—these are just some of the logistical problems that can destroy the effectiveness of a meeting. If the meeting is not in your offices, always check out the room before you book it. Make sure that it is not next to the kitchen, a bar, a casino, or a freeway. Carefully evaluate the layout, lighting, sound system, and ventilation. Many ballrooms that you might book for a meeting were actually designed as banquet rooms with "nightclub lighting," which means that the light levels are too low for people to comfortably take notes and pay attention to the speaker at the front of the room. After complaining and being stonewalled by hotels, we have had to actually call outside suppliers, rent supplementary lighting and speaker systems, and then pay extra for the right setup.

Always visit the meeting site in advance to make sure that the room and facilities are set up exactly as you had agreed. On the day of the event, recheck the meeting room at least one hour before the meeting is to be held. On numerous occasions, hotel people have told us that the room was being used and that we could not see it the day before the function because they would not be setting up until 1:00 a.m. We then made arrangements to be there at 1:00 a.m. to make sure that the room was set up exactly as we had requested. Almost without exception, they were setting it up incorrectly. (I will talk in detail about the importance of logistics in Chapter 16.)

ELEVEN

One-on-One Meetings

THERE IS a direct relationship between how freely an individual can speak to his or her boss and the productivity and the creativity of the employee. The more freely employees can speak and express their ideas and opinions, the more relaxed and confident they are about their work, and the better work they do.

The only way to develop this friendly feeling between the boss and staff members is to have regular conversations that go back and forth in a relaxed and supportive environment. The one-on-one meeting is one of the very best ways for managers to create this type of high-performance environment with and among their staff members. There is nothing like it.

Goal Setting and Review

Cameron Herold, author of *Double Double*, calls this a "goal setting and review meeting." This is a good description. When you meet with each of your team members on a weekly basis, you get an opportunity to discuss his/her goals and activities and be updated on the work that the person is doing, and how well everything is going.

This information sharing is then also a teaching and learning opportunity, which enables you to give both guidance and mentoring to your team members to help them perform at their best.

Andrew Grove of Intel wrote that the one-on-one meeting was one of the most important responsibilities of managerial life. His opinion was that a manager should hold these one-hour meetings once a week with each direct report. He also felt that no manager should have more than twelve to fifteen people reporting to him, or all his time would be taken up in these meetings.

Like other effective meetings, the one-on-one meeting has a written agenda that both parties follow. This agenda is prepared by the team member with a list of discussion items, concerns, or problems that have come up in the team member's area of responsibility. This agenda also includes the goals or activities that the team member is working on, as well as a progress report.

Ask Questions and Listen Carefully

The best way to manage this type of meeting is for you to ask good questions and listen intently to the answers. A common weakness of managers is that they often have an irresistible urge to contribute their knowledge and wisdom the very first moment the employee may be in need of it. You should resist this temptation. Ask questions instead, starting with, "How is everything going?"

There is a rule that "the person who asks questions has control." When you ask open-ended questions beginning with words such as *how, when, who,* and *which,* none of which can be answered with a simple yes or no, you give the employee an opportunity to open up and expand in that area.

One of the most powerful questions you can ask when your employee presents you with a problem or a dilemma is, "What do you think you should do?"

Avoid Making Decisions

When you give advice to people and tell them what you think they should do, you are actually making them dependent on you. You are setting them up to feel uncomfortable and insecure if they act without seeking your advice again.

Draw Out Their Best Thinking

Instead, continue to ask, "What do you think?" It is quite amazing how many of your staff members have already made a decision about what to do, but they are not 100 percent sure. When they tell you what they think needs to be done, you can tell them that you think it is an excellent idea. If necessary, you can then suggest something else that the employee might do as well.

The best length for a one-on-one meeting is between sixty and ninety minutes. Schedule the meeting well in advance, even from week to week, on a particular day and at a particular time. At this time, turn off your phone and have your calls held. Put your computer on silent so that there are no electronic interruptions during the conversation.

It is helpful if you sit at a table, corner to corner, rather than directly across a desk, which always is felt as an invisible barrier between two people. Something as simple as offering the employee a cup of coffee or a glass of water before you get started can have an amazingly positive effect on the tone of the meeting.

As Andrew Grove said, meeting one-on-one, face-to-face, knee-to-knee, and preferably weekly with each of the people reporting to you is one of your most important responsibilities as a manager.

A Career Changer

One of the most powerful influences in my life was when I worked for the Big Boss of a conglomerate. I always worked late and was often the only employee of the 200 people in the head office who was still working at 6:00 p.m. As it happened, the Big Boss would often be at his desk as well.

One evening, he phoned me in my office, having seen that my light was still on, and invited me to come down to his office for a chat, which I did. This invitation led to the development of a warm relationship that had me staying late after work almost every night, with the boss regularly inviting me down to his office for a thirty- to sixty-minute discussion four or five days a week. Those evening meetings were the most wonderful mentoring experiences of my young business life. His taking the time to talk to me and share his ideas with me made me a better person for the rest of my career.

You can have this same effect on each person who reports to you. Resolve today to schedule a personal meeting with each of your direct reports. In fact, move it up on your list of priorities to make it one of the most important things you do as a manager, and as a person.

TWELVE

Meetings for Delegating Assignments

ONE OF your most important skills for success in management is your ability to delegate assignments in the right way to the right people. These one-on-one or small group meetings can be some of the most important work that you ever do.

Effective delegation meetings can free up an enormous amount of your time to do more productive work and to do the work that only you can do.

Your ability to delegate effectively to others is the key to leveraging yourself and multiplying your value to your company. Without the ability to delegate effectively, you will find it is impossible to move up or to advance in management to higher positions of responsibility.

The Starting Point

The starting point of delegation is for you to think through the job. What exactly needs to be done? To what standard does it need to be done? What is the required date of completion?

Often, a simple job does not need to be done by a more experienced and valuable person. You assign tasks based on the knowledge, skill, and hourly income of the person you want to do the job.

Choose the Right Person

Once you are clear about the job that needs to be done, you then select the right person to do the job and arrange a meeting with that person. Match the requirements of the job to the abilities of the person. When you delegate the job to the right person, you are then free to focus your attention on other things.

The more responsibilities that you give to people, the stronger and more positive they become. When you sit down with someone and delegate the entire job to that employee, this responsibility becomes a major motivator of performance.

Explain Clearly

Explain exactly what you want done—the how, the what, and the why of the task. Explain clearly the outcomes and results that are required. Make these results measurable.

Especially, in this type of one-on-one meeting, invite participation and encourage discussion. The more opportunity that employees have to discuss a job with the boss before they begin, the more committed they will be to completing the task, to the required standard and on schedule. There seems to be a one-to-one relationship between how much people get to talk about the job and how much they understand it, accept it, and are committed to doing it.

The more your employees and team members can discuss the job, the more they internalize ownership of the job and see doing the job as something that is personal to them rather than simply helpful to the company.

Ask for Feedback

Once you have explained the job, what needs to be done and when, and to what standard, ask the other person to feed it back to you in his own words. When delegating a job, never assume that the other person understood exactly what you asked him to do.

This was a lesson I learned as a young manager. I was astonished to find that, even after I had clearly assigned a specific job to a specific person, either the job was not done well or it was not done at all. Often the staff member left the meeting unsure about the exact job to be done; as a result, the worker was paralyzed, like a deer in the headlights, and did nothing at all. To my amazement, even after a thirty- or sixty-minute conversation, in fully 50 percent of cases, the other person had misheard or misremembered what we just talked about.

Ever after, I learned to always ask others to feed back to me, in their own words, exactly what I had asked them to do.

Set a Deadline and Schedule

Once you and the delegatee are clear about the task to be done, set a clear deadline and sub-deadlines on every task. An assignment without a deadline is merely a discussion.

Remember that *delegation is not abdication*. Even though you are assigning someone to do the job, you are still accountable for whether the job is done properly and on schedule.

Next set a schedule for reporting. This reporting can be a part of your weekly one-on-one meetings, or it can be a separate communication, either delivered personally or by e-mail. When your employees know that they have to meet or talk with you on a regular basis about the progress of the job, they are much more likely to do the job on schedule, much to the benefit of the company, and to themselves personally as well.

Finally, once you have delegated the job, express your confidence in your staff. Tell them that you are sure that they will do a great job and that you look forward to seeing how everything works out. An expression of confident expectations by the boss in the staff member is one of the most powerful of all motivations for excellent work.

This final statement of confidence is often the motivating spark that causes a person to take ownership of the assignment and to commit internally to doing an excellent job. After this kind of meeting, if you handle it properly, you can then turn your attention to other things with a high degree of assurance that the job will be done on time and as you expected.

THIRTEEN

Meetings Outside the Office

AN ENORMOUS amount of your time in your business life will be spent at meetings outside of your own office or home turf. You will be holding business meetings in other people's territory, at the offices of customers, suppliers, bankers, lawyers, and accountants or at branch offices of your own company. In these cases, where you do not control the environment, you must exert whatever control is available to you.

Just as you plan and prepare for your internal meetings, you must plan and prepare for external meetings as well, and sometimes even more so. Always define the purpose of the meeting in advance with the other person who is setting up the meeting. I say something like, "I know how busy you are. To make sure that we use our time to its very highest and best value, let's take a couple of minutes to agree on what it is we want to accomplish at this meeting."

Get Clarity in Advance

Don't fall into the trap of traveling to a meeting somewhere in your city, or in another city, and then asking, "Well, what is our purpose for being here?"

Before attending any meeting outside the office, call whoever is arranging the meeting and ask about the reasons so that you can prepare thoroughly and bring everything you need to make this meeting effective. Do your reading. Pack the necessary materials. Remember that this is an expensive use of your time, especially if you have to travel any distance.

Restate the Purpose

When the outside meeting begins, restate the purpose of the meeting so that you are all on the same page. One of the questions that I ask when I start an outside meeting is, "Before we start, tell me ideally what you would like us to accomplish in this meeting."

Some time ago, I flew to Chicago for an all-day meeting. It was to be a discussion of new products and negotiations over how much would be paid to which party and for what. I flew in the night before. We had allocated six to eight hours the following day to go through several pages of items and contract clauses.

On the plane, I wrote out a list of everything I thought that my counterparts in the negotiation would want to accomplish. I then wrote out a list of everything that I wanted to achieve, if I could. I was thoroughly prepared.

Define the Perfect Outcome

When we sat down at 9:00 a.m. in their offices, I told them about my preparations. I asked them, "If the outcome of this meeting was perfect, what would you like to see accomplished?"

They had been expecting a long, complex negotiation. However, when I asked them this question, they opened up immediately and told me exactly what their situation was and what they wanted to accomplish. I compared their requests with my notes and found that we only had about three or four areas of difference. Everything else was mutually agreeable.

So instead of going through the many pages of contract provisions, we focused on the three or four areas of difference, quickly reached agreement, and concluded a very successful negotiation by 11:00 a.m. The agreement that we entered into lasted for many years and was the basis of a large amount of additional business that we engaged in together. And it took only two hours.

The Physical Environment

One final point. Do everything possible to control the physical environment when you are meeting in the offices of someone else. Sit with your back to a wall rather than to the doorway. Sit where you can look straight into the face of the key person with whom you are meeting. Be prepared, professional, and polished. Take the meeting seriously, but not yourself.

Some of the most important meetings in your life and career will occur in the meeting rooms and offices of other people, sometimes at great distance. Your willingness and ability to prepare thoroughly for each of these meetings can have a major impact on your future.

Determine the Timing

Agree on a time length for the meeting: "Let's agree on a time for us to finish. I estimate that we should be done with this discussion by 11:30. Is that agreeable to you?"

Once you have agreed to the time, you can go beyond it if necessary, but a specific time is a "forcing system" that presses you to closure, like the reverse of Parkinson's Law.

Stay on track. Try to avoid deviating onto other subjects, even if you are not in charge of the meeting. Sometimes, when people start speaking about different subjects, I will gently smile and say, "Moving right along now. . . ." This helps people get back onto the subject being discussed.

Press for Closure

Bring each item to a conclusion and then move on. At the end of the meeting, summarize what each person is going to do, and when, and to what standard. Press for closure.

Keep good and complete notes in each meeting. The power is always on the side of the person with the best notes. It is amazing how people often forget what was agreed on; the person who took careful notes then has considerable power in what happens later.

Many of the most important turning points in your career will be determined by what you do, or fail to do, in meetings held in the offices and facilities of other people. Your willingness and ability to prepare thoroughly for these meetings can have a major impact on your career.

FOURTEEN

Organize the Meeting Facilities — Internal

YOUR CHOICE of a location for a small or large group meeting can be an essential factor in its success. Over the years, I have given or presented at more than 5,000 talks and seminars, with the smallest group being seven and the largest group being 25,000. Here's what I have learned: Prior Proper Preparation Prevents Poor Performance.

It seems that in many areas of life, including speaking engagements, meetings, days in court, sales presentations, and so on, 90 percent of success is determined by preparation.

Over-Prepare?

A wealthy and successful lawyer once asked me to testify in a case that he was handling. He brought me a box full of files and depositions and asked me if I would glance through them quickly so that I would have an idea of what kind of questions would be asked of me.

I promised him that I would read through the entire box carefully and take notes. I told him that I believed in over-preparing.

He smiled knowingly and said something that I'll never forgot: "I do not believe there is such a word as 'over-prepare.'"

Nonetheless, it applies to meeting facilities of all kinds, every time.

Never Assume

Robert Burns, the Scottish poet, once said, "The best laid schemes of mice and men gang aft agley [often go wrong]."

One of these places where they *gang aft agley* is when we assume that the meeting room is going to be set up exactly right. We then arrive to find that the air-conditioning is broken, the lights don't work properly, the overhead projector and computer are not hooked up correctly, and there are insufficient chairs for the people attending the meeting.

The key to avoiding this is to always "over-prepare."

Start with the Room

When we hold a public seminar of any kind, the very first thing we need to do is to find the right meeting room. Over the years, we have had to delay, postpone, and even cancel seminars because we could not find a single meeting room to accommodate our needs, even in a large city. Only when we have the meeting room nailed down do we begin seminar preparations and marketing.

In arranging an internal meeting facility, your first task is checking that the room you need is available. If you work in a large office, the worst thing that can happen is to have several people agree to meet and then find out that the only room available is being used by someone else at that time.

Make sure that whoever schedules the space knows that you are going to be using it at a specific time. Make sure there has been no double booking. It was Peter Drucker who said, "Errant assumptions lie at the root of every failure."

Check It Out

Go and check out the room personally. Inspect it carefully and make sure that it has everything you need to conduct the kind of meeting that you are planning.

Perhaps one of the best meeting management tools ever created is the *checklist.* The checklist consists of a written list of every step and requirement to conduct a specific meeting at a specific time. This checklist is organized by sequence, from the first step all the way through to the last. It then becomes the blueprint for the meeting and is adhered to religiously by everyone sharing the responsibility to ensure that the meeting goes smoothly.

Think about the proper layout for an effective meeting. Arrange for the necessary chairs, tables, and other essential facilities to be brought in. Your goal is for the meeting attendees to be so comfortable that they are actually unaware of their surroundings. This enables them to concentrate completely on the business of the meeting, without being distracted by some unexpected problem such as a broken air-conditioning system.

Knowledge Workers

Another of my favorite observations by Drucker is: "The most valuable asset in the company is executive thinking time."

When you bring several people into a room, you are actually bringing their brains and their ability to express their thinking into the room. You want to make sure that there are no obstacles to the fully functioning of the best thinking of every meeting participant.

Make sure the meeting room has proper lighting and ventilation. According to the studies on ergonomics, 68 degrees Fahrenheit is the ideal meeting room temperature. Just as a microprocessor in a computer functions best at the right temperature, 68 degrees is the best thinking temperature for the business brain.

Think About Layout

Give some thought to room layout, too. At the best meetings, at the best organizations with which I have worked, every participant has a name tag. These name tags are set out in specific places at the tables where the participants are going to sit. The organizers have taken the time to think carefully about who should be on the right side and the left side of each participant, who should be sitting directly across the table, and how far each participant should be from the person conducting the meeting at the head of the table. You should do the same.

Be sure to provide coffee and whatever other refreshments are appropriate, especially if the meeting is going to go beyond one or two hours. You don't want people having to wander around the office to find coffee and then hauling it back to the meeting so that they have something in front of them. You should have the beverages and the food in the back of the room, or just outside the room, so that people don't have to travel any distance to get it.

Cut off outside interruptions, whenever possible. Do not allow anyone to come in and interrupt during the course of the meeting. Start the meeting punctually. Close the door, call the meeting to order, and begin at the appointed time.

FIFTEEN

Organize the Meeting Facilities—External

AN IMPORTANT executive skill is the ability to arrange and coordinate meetings in hotel rooms or other meeting facilities away from the office.

When you start off in management, it seldom occurs to you that one of the most important events in your career can be organizing a major meeting. This responsibility is often dumped on you unexpectedly. Your boss decides that you need to have a large company meeting, seminar, convention, workshop, or some other function that brings together a large number of people. He then asks if you will just "take care of it."

Good or Bad Meeting?

When I was a manager, I attended hundreds of meetings of all sizes, at all levels of quality, all over the country and all over the world. I had an excellent opportunity to get a sense of what constituted a good meeting and what constituted a bad or poorly planned meeting.

When I began giving seminars of my own (by now more than 1,000 worldwide), I got a brand-new education in the complexities of setting up large and small meetings in rented or borrowed facilities.

Eventually, we developed a 104-page workbook/checklist to ensure that every single detail necessary to the proper functioning of a large meeting was thought through, checked, and double-checked. Because these meetings involved my livelihood, and a loss on a publicly promoted seminar could be disastrous for a small business, I read everything I could find on the proper conduct of such meetings.

Study the Contract

Remember, the people you are talking to at the hotel or seminar center are not your friends. They have taken courses to learn how to be smiling and charming throughout the discussion. But everything they do is aimed at getting you to sign a contract that obligates you to pay the maximum amount humanly possible for use of their meeting facilities, and even more than that, if possible.

Begin with the contract. This is the bible of the banquet or meeting industry. This is the ironclad agreement by which hotels operate, and they want you to sign it, preferably as soon as possible, and back it up with a hefty, nonrefundable deposit.

Either you or someone else should read every clause and sub-clause. The contract is almost always a minefield of paragraphs where there are *additional* charges. Remember, they only have one opportunity to soak you as much as possible, so they are going to use every artifice and trick possible to extract as much money out of you that they can at this time.

The most common way of extracting money from innocent businesspeople organizing hotel functions is getting them to commit to a minimum number of room nights. You must resist this ploy at all costs. If necessary, book the minimum number of nights and demand the right to reduce the room commitment as you get closer to the meeting or conference.

The next way that hotels overcharge you is by selling you endless numbers of refreshments. Commit to a minimum number of refreshments in advance, and then maintain the option to increase the quantities as you get closer to the date of the function.

View the Room Personally

Never book a facility over the phone and simply assume that it is going to be fine. Leave nothing to chance. Be sure to go to the meeting facility or hotel personally and walk through every part of the venue. Go and inspect the room, walking all around to get a sense of how it is laid out and what obstacles to sight there might be, like posts and columns. Find out what will be happening next door. Find out what functions are booked in the adjoining rooms at the same time as your meeting. How many people will be there? What level of sound can you expect from the adjoining rooms?

A Meeting Disaster

On one occasion, we rented a large banquet room with sufficient seminar space for 400 people, with tables, chairs, a stage, a sound system, and podium. What they didn't tell us was that they had rented the adjoining room for a large wedding that evening; the reception started at 5:00 p.m., but the band was scheduled to set up and practice from 2:00 p.m. onward, which they did.

I still remember trying to conduct a business seminar with a rock band practicing full blast in the adjoining room, literally knocking us out of our chairs. When we complained to the hotel, the facility's event planners smiled innocently and told us that there was nothing they could do. It seemed they had no idea that we needed a quiet environment for a business seminar so that the speaker at our meeting could be heard.

In another case, we organized an evening meeting for about 100 people in a downtown hotel. What the hotel staff didn't tell us was that a nightclub with a paper-thin wall was next to our meeting room, and the nightclub started up with a rock band at 7:00 p.m. We had to shout to make ourselves heard over the din.

The Big Three

There are three things that can go wrong at a meeting or function of any kind. In order, they are *sound, light,* and *air-conditioning.* To guard against problems in these three areas, check out the sound system thoroughly, and be sure that people can hear clearly from every place in the room.

Second, check the lighting. Make sure there's enough light for people to take notes and generally be comfortable in a business seminar where presentations are being given. Most especially, be sure that there is a lot of light on the stage and on the face of the speaker.

Third, check out the room temperature. Lack of air-conditioning can ruin a big meeting. Some friends of mine who gave seminars all over the country would write into the contract that the rooms must be kept at 68 degrees Fahrenheit or the rent would be free—no charge.

There are few accomplishments that will get you more accolades and respect from your superiors than your putting together an excellent business meeting for your company or department. Many people I have worked with have reported being promoted, paid more, and moved onto the fast track in their companies after having organized an excellent meeting.

SIXTEEN

Room Layout
for Meetings

THE WAY A room is laid out can make a major difference in the effectiveness of a meeting and your presentation. When you are leading a small meeting and are using a round or rectangular table, position yourself opposite the entrance so that the participants are facing you and have their backs to latecomers and other interruptions. This is the "power position," where you can visually *control* the whole room.

If you are a participant in a meeting, the power position for you is close to and facing the leader so that you are able to make eye contact with the most important person. In this position, you are also able to see the entire room and the entrance. Go to the meeting early so that you can be sure to get one of the best places—a place where you can have the greatest influence on the meeting organizer, usually the boss, and on the meeting participants themselves.

Everything Counts

For medium-size meetings (made up of about 15–25 people), a horseshoe-shaped or box-shaped setting is ideal to ensure maximum group eye contact and relaxed interaction. This is one of my favorite layouts for a larger meeting as well, whenever possible. In every case, you want to be sitting at the "top of the curve." You always want to be facing the entrance, either as the meeting leader or as a participant.

Eye Contact

Whenever possible, arrange the chairs and tables so that people can see each other's faces, rather than the back of someone's head. It is quite amazing how quickly people warm up, relax, and become spontaneous and friendly when they can look around the room with a small turn of the head and see the faces of more than half of the other people in attendance.

Another layout you can use for large group presentations is the chevron style. This is where you lay out the chairs in a V shape with people seated at an angle, both to you and the stage, on the one side, and to the other participants, on the other. Although the participants cannot see all of the other attendees without twisting or turning, they have eye contact with a large number of people. They can see when other people smile, nod their heads, laugh, clap, or participate in any way. This has a multiplier effect, generating and increasing the participation of each of the other people.

Theater Style

The least effective layout when setting up chairs in a large meeting room is theater style. This is where the rows are straight across, with everyone facing forward and everyone not in the front row looking at the back of the head of the person in front of them. This layout is unavoidable for large meetings, but it is not the best choice if you want everyone to relax, communicate, and participate emotionally and intellectually in the meeting.

There is no such thing as too much preparation when it comes to putting on a large meeting. Too much is at stake. Too many people's feelings and opinions can be affected. Go to the room early and walk all around the room while it is still empty. If there is anything that you are not happy with, insist that it be changed immediately. Don't be afraid to speak up.

Get Them Close

When I give seminars, I want the front row of chairs to be so close that I can reach out from the edge of the stage and touch a person in the front row. For some reason, hotels will often put a twenty- to thirty-foot gap between the stage and the first row of participants. This makes it much harder for speakers to develop rapport and trust with the audience. I call it the "talk across the street" way of setting up the room.

Whenever I come into a room and see this setup, I immediately insist that the hotel find as many people as necessary to take the chairs from the back rows and bring them forward to create rows in the front. Of course, the hotel people always resist. They do not want to change anything or make any additional efforts. Your job is to insist that it be done correctly, exactly as you requested when you booked the room.

Here is an important point: When you book the room, sit with the organizers and draw out a diagram on paper to indicate exactly where you want the chairs and tables to be relative to the stage. Remember, the people who set up the room do not necessarily speak English. Nor do they particularly care whether or not the room setup is consistent with the contractual arrangements. They often come in overnight to set up the room and are gone by the time you arrive. This is neither right nor wrong; it is just the way it is.

Avoid Distractions

With regard to rooms that have windows that are open to the outside, there are some special notes. First of all, the windows should be curtained or shaded in some way so that people cannot look outside to see other people and cars going by. Be sure that they do not have big windows with a beautiful view, attractive features, or hotel activities going on to the sides or behind you. This kind of distraction can ruin your presentation because you will usually lose the attention of your audience.

On one occasion, I was one of four speakers giving a seminar at a Florida hotel. The meeting room was beautiful in every respect except one: the location. The hotel had an Olympic-size pool and the meeting room jutted out partially as if hovering over the pool. The stage for the speaker was in front of a window that directly overlooked the swimming pool beyond. They had opened the curtains so that the room was flooded with light on all sides, making it difficult to see the speaker's face. But the worst part of all was that there was a large beauty contest being conducted at this hotel on this very weekend. At least fifty of the contestants were playing and splashing in the water on both sides of this meeting room and behind the speaker, virtually all wearing skimpy bathing suits and big beauty contest smiles.

No One Was Listening

The conference speakers gave their presentations competing against this attractive backdrop of beauty contestants splashing in the pool. They might as well have stayed in their rooms and spoken to themselves. No one was paying any attention to them. Before I got up to speak, I asked the hotel staff to close the curtains on three sides, which they did. For the first time, the speaker had the entire attention of the audience. I never forgot that experience.

SEVENTEEN

Making Presentations at Meetings

THE PRESENTATION is one of the most important of all tools for the executive. Many individuals change their minds and many companies change their strategies as the result of an effective presentation by a well-prepared person. A good presentation gives you an opportunity to demonstrate competence, preparation, knowledge, expertise, and command of your subject. Because of their potential importance to your future, effective presentations cannot be left to chance.

Present to Persuade

It has been said that the course of human destiny is affected more by the spoken word than by any other influence. It is changed by the individual standing (or sitting) and presenting in such a way that people are persuaded to think, feel, and act differently than they would have in the absence of the presentation.

Think of a presentation as a speech or oration, only with smaller groups and greater audience participation. In a speech, you open with words that set the stage, gain the attention of the audience, and point in the direction in which you are going. When you open your presentation, everyone in the room should know what you are going to be talking about.

You then develop your presentation in stages, one point at a time, each point leading logically into the next point. Whenever possible, use examples and illustrations to prove your points or drive them deeper.

The Job to Be Done

Each talk or presentation has a job to do. The purpose of your making a presentation is to make a sale of some kind. It is to get people to take action on your suggestions that they would not have taken if they had not heard you speak.

Plan your opening word for word, and rehearse it over and over again in your mind, aloud, and in front of a mirror. Your opening comments set the stage, build expectations, and communicate a clear message to your audience.

In the course of giving your talk, you should think about the visual elements that you can use to illustrate your points and make them come alive for the meeting participants.

PowerPoint in Speaking

Whether you use PowerPoint depends on many factors. Many presenters at meetings have started to rely on PowerPoint presentations so heavily that their personalities and the essence of their talks get lost as they go from point to point on the screen.

If you are going to use PowerPoint, which can be ideal in certain situations, it is best to follow a few rules.

The 5 Times 5 Rule

First and foremost, you should never have more than five lines of text on a slide, and each line should not have more than five words. Any more than this can distract and even confuse your audience. The exception is that with a smaller room or group, you can use more lines or words than the rule permits.

Regardless of how many points you use, bring them up one at a time as you are commenting on them. Don't make the mistake of bringing up the entire slide full of information so that the participants are busy reading and not paying any attention to you.

Too Much Information

Not long ago, I had a speaking engagement with a multinational company. The president spoke to the 250-person group for an hour before it was my turn to speak. His PowerPoint presentation consisted of a single slide with hundreds of numbers in rows and columns, none of which were clear or legible to anyone in the audience. He spoke to the screen, commenting on the numbers, for a full hour. Because he was the president, everyone in the room sat politely, but it was excruciatingly painful for all the participants.

Face the Audience

Face the audience when you use PowerPoint. You should have your laptop or tablet in front of you illustrating what is on the screen behind you. As you click through your PowerPoint presentation, keep your eyes on the meeting participants and speak to them the whole time.

When you are not referring to a point on the screen, push the B on your laptop's keyboard to blank out the screen. Remember, your face is the most important element in any presentation, and while there are words on the screen, people's eyes will be darting from your face to the screen and back again, like spectators at a tennis match.

Lights Please

When you use PowerPoint, it is essential that your face be well lit throughout. I am continually dismayed when I see senior executives delivering their presentation in the dark in order to assure maximum clarity for the projector and the screen. Remember, you are the "star" of the presentation, not the words on the screen.

PowerPoint Is Only a Prop

Only use PowerPoint as a prop or as a support tool. It should not be the main focus of the talk. You are the main focus of the presentation—the essential human element—and PowerPoint is there merely to assist you and to illustrate your points more clearly to the audience.

When you use PowerPoint, practice and rehearse. Go through a dry run three to five times before you make your presentation. Do a complete dress rehearsal to ensure that the PowerPoint program and the projector are properly connected and working smoothly before you stand up to speak.

Expect the Unexpected

You have probably seen or been in situations where the entire talk is built around PowerPoint and then PowerPoint somehow fails to function. The speaker begins clicking and nothing happens. The presentation grinds to a halt while everyone stands around looking sheepish and foolish—especially you.

Keep the Attention on You and Your Message

In every case, when you use PowerPoint, start off with a strong, clear statement that sets the stage for your presentation. You can then use PowerPoint to illustrate critical numbers, points, and relationships. When you have finished your PowerPoint presentation, blank out the screen and be sure to face your audience and end with a strong verbal message, your call to action.

Flipcharts and Whiteboards

Instead of PowerPoint, you can also use flipcharts or whiteboards. But never forget that the focus must be on your face, gestures, and words. If you use a flipchart, prepare it in advance by writing your key points in pencil on the sheets. This penciled-in information will be invisible to the audience but will allow you to write clearly and authoritatively, as if from memory.

When you use a flipchart, after you have made your point and people have had a chance to absorb the words, numbers, or illustrations that you have written or drawn, turn the page over so that you once more have a blank page. This helps the audience to refocus on you.

Another way to use a flipchart is to write out your key points in advance on alternate pages. Be sure you have a clean sheet facing the audience before you begin. When you go to the flipchart for the first time, turn over the clean sheet and there will be your first set of points. When you turn over this sheet, there will be a second clean sheet covering up the next set of points.

If you use a whiteboard, after you have finished with each key point, erase it so that the whiteboard is once again blank. Otherwise, your audience's eyes will be flicking back and forth like a windshield wiper, between you and the words on the board. In every case, you want the audience to come back to your face without being distracted by what is written or projected on the page, board, or screen.

Be sure to provide your own markers and pens, too. You would be amazed how often this detail is overlooked and the pens are either dried out and unusable, or someone has forgotten to provide them at all.

Practice Makes Perfect

A final key point with regard to presentation tools of all kinds, PowerPoint, flipchart, or whiteboard, is to practice, practice, practice. If it is important to you and to the audience, go through it again and again. Run through it in advance, preferably with a small audience. Remember that one great presentation can advance your career, make you a star, and put you onto the fast track. Don't miss an opportunity to make an excellent presentation.

EIGHTEEN

Developing Self-Confidence in Meetings

ACCORDING TO the Guinness Book of Lists, 54 percent of adults put the fear of public speaking ahead of the fear of death among life's greatest fears. This applies to people participating in meetings and speaking up in front of their peers. In many cases, people are so shy and fearful that they sit quietly throughout the meeting, hoping not to be noticed.

Sometimes I start my presentations by telling my audience that the fear of public speaking is one of the most traumatic fears of all and that it often holds people back from achieving all that is possible for them. I tell them, "Let me demonstrate this fear and how it holds people back."

I then say, "Later in this presentation, I am going to pick someone from the audience to come up here on the stage and give us a short presentation on what they have learned and what they are going to do differently as a result of this talk."

I let my eyes sweep over the audience, going from person to person as though I am trying to decide which of these audience participants I will bring up onto the stage to speak. The audience will go dead silent. I will then ask, "How did you feel when I told you that I might be calling you up here to speak in front of this audience?"

Most people will say, "I sure hope it isn't me!"

Speaking Can Be Terrifying

The very thought of having to stand up and speak in front of your peers, or even worse, an audience of strangers, can be traumatizing. Your stomach will churn. Your heart will race. Your mind will go blank. You will begin to sweat.

However, your ability to speak up and speak clearly, to make your point and to persuade others to your point of view, can accelerate your career and put you onto the fast track in your company.

You need to make a decision to overcome shyness or the fear of public speaking. You must make a business decision to become excellent at speaking in front of other people.

Do What You Fear

Ralph Waldo Emerson talks about walking down the street in Concord, Massachusetts, as a young man. A piece of paper blew against his leg. He reached down, picked it up, and read the words, "Do the thing you fear, and the death of fear is certain." Emerson said that those words changed his life.

In psychology, we know that the only way for you to overcome a fear of any kind is to do what you are afraid to do. Very often, your greatest success lies on the other side of your greatest fear. If you can push through it, not only can you be even more successful, but you can eliminate other fears that may be holding you back as well.

Toastmasters or Dale Carnegie

The way that you overcome the fear of speaking up in meetings is to join a local chapter of Toastmasters International or to take a Dale Carnegie course in public speaking. I have met people all over the world who have transformed their lives in just a few weeks by attending these meetings and getting an opportunity to speak at them.

This is called the "process of systematic desensitization." When you do something over and over again, eventually you lose your fear of doing it. When you join one of these organizations, you will have an opportunity to stand up and say a few words each week to the other members of your group. At first, you may be nervous and fearful. But after the second or third week, you find yourself speaking in front of people, each of whom you know by their first name. It is like a small "business family." Your fear goes away.

The Inverse Relationship

There is an inverse relationship between fear and self-confidence. As your self-confidence increases as the result of your successful experiences, your fear goes down in equal proportion. Soon you reach the point where you are totally unafraid to speak up and express yourself with any group, on almost any subject.

In addition, there are many good books and audio courses on public speaking. The improvements can be quick and permanent. Within six months of beginning to learn to speak by attending regular meetings, and both reading and listening to books and audios on the subject, you will be able to speak up in front of an audience of any kind, and speak with both confidence and clarity.

The Speaker's Academy

In our Speaker's Academy, we teach people how to prepare mentally and emotionally for an upcoming talk or presentation. The most important part of preparation is visualization.

You create a clear mental picture of yourself speaking calmly and confidently in front of your peers, and you replay this picture on the screen of your mind over and over again until it is accepted as a template by your subconscious mind. Then, the next time you find yourself in a meeting, your subconscious mind will show you the confidence and courage you need to turn your inner picture into your outer reality.

Speak Up at Meetings

There is a rule that the people who speak first in a meeting usually end up having the greatest influence on the outcome of the meeting as it proceeds. This is why you should resolve to speak up clearly within five minutes of the beginning of the meeting, whatever the subject.

Remember the old adage: The person who asks questions has control. By asking a clear question of the meeting leader, or of another key person who is making a point, you can establish yourself as thoughtful, intelligent, and fully engaged in the meeting. By asking a good question, people see you as a "player" in the meeting. In addition, the person of whom you are asking the question sees you as an important person and influence and will often begin to address you regularly throughout the meeting to ensure your understanding and support.

An advantage of speaking up early in the meeting is that thereafter you will be far more confident in speaking up whenever you have a question or observation.

There is another rule that says, "The person who does not contribute to a meeting is considered to have nothing to contribute." When someone sits quietly in a meeting because they are too shy or insecure to speak up, eventually the other participants at the meeting conclude that this person has nothing of value to add to the subject. This is not a perception that you wish to project.

One final point: When you develop the ability to speak confidently and competently on your feet, without even realizing it you develop far higher levels of confidence and competence when it comes to speaking one-on-one or in any kind of meeting within your business or organization. This ability increases your level of self-confidence and self-assurance in every interaction with other people, in your personal life and in business.

NINETEEN

Parkinson's Law in Meetings

SOME YEARS ago a British bureaucrat, C. Northcote Parkinson, wrote a little book called *Parkinson's Law: The Pursuit of Progress*. This book has had a profound influence on millions of people over the decades.

Parkinson's Law says that "work expands to fill the time available for its completion." So, if you have eight hours to complete a list of tasks, you will take the full eight hours to complete the tasks and will still be rushing at the end of the day.

What Parkinson noted, in studying the British civil service, was that no matter how many people were hired and how large the departments became, everyone was busy all day long, even if very little was actually being accomplished. This is one of the great weaknesses of bureaucracies of all kinds, but especially government bureaucracies.

Parkinson at Meetings

This law applies especially to meetings. Meetings expand to fill the time allotted for them. If you allocate two hours to cover the agenda at a meeting, it will take the full two hours, and you will be rushing at the end, and often making poor decisions, to finish the meeting. But if you allocate only one hour to cover the same number of agenda items, you will quite surprisingly finish up within one hour.

The rule is to "start on time and end early." Announce a start time. Assume the latecomer is not coming and begin. Move quickly from point to point as you go through the agenda. Don't get off track or waste time on other issues.

Break the Law

Your goal is to challenge yourself to break Parkinson's Law. Set a specific time for the discussion of each item on the agenda. When you hand out the agenda, note the time that will be spent in the right-hand margin, such as 9:00–9:10. This is a not-so-subtle way of getting people to get to the point and to avoid digressing into other subjects.

When people realize that the time allocated for the meeting or for the discussion of a particular item in the meeting is limited, they will be much more likely to get right to the point, and stay on point.

Allocate Your Time

You can also use this breaking of Parkinson's Law in every other part of your work and planning. When someone calls you on the phone or drops by and wants to talk to you, you immediately respond by saying, "I have a call coming in eight minutes from now." Or, "I have exactly eleven minutes to talk to you before I have to leave."

Many of the most effective executives I work with will tell me upfront that they have only a specific number of minutes to talk, so—can we get right to the point?

A person who would normally take thirty or forty minutes to speak will get right to the point in the first two minutes. Very often these people will cover everything on their agendas in just a few minutes.

Set a Deadline

The best thing you can do, if you find yourself with talkative people who tend to drag out meetings, is to say that you must all be out of there in sixteen minutes. An odd time really intimidates people. And as you approach the deadline that you have announced, begin folding up your materials and putting them away in preparation to leave. People will get to the point and stay on the point quite quickly under these circumstances.

You can use this technique yourself to dramatically increase both your efficiency and your effectiveness. Give yourself tight deadlines to complete important tasks. You will be amazed at how much you can get done when you give yourself a cutoff time when you will have to leave or go on to something else.

TWENTY

Tips for Personal Meeting Effectiveness

THERE ARE several things you can do to make meetings more effective. The first, of course, is to have an agenda. One of the best ways to organize your agenda is to discuss the agenda items in advance with the other people who will be at the meeting.

The rule should be "no surprises!" Give the attendees as much advance knowledge and information on the subject of the meeting as you possibly can. Allow them an opportunity to prepare and organize their thoughts. When they come into the meeting, they should have a good idea of what is going to be discussed and what the goals of the meeting might be.

Clarity of Purpose

Start the meeting with a clear statement of purpose. Say something like, "This meeting is to decide whether or not we are going to increase the budget in this area, and if so, by how much, and if we are going to reduce the budget, how much should that be?"

My friend Joel Weldon, one of the top professional speakers and teachers of professional speakers, uses a particular example to illustrate this point. He calls it the "sign on the bus."

He points out that if you are standing at a bus stop waiting to catch a bus from point A to point B, how do you decide which bus to get on? The answer, of course, is the bus that has your destination written on the sign above the driver.

By the same token, a great way to increase personal efficiency in a meeting or presentation of any kind is for you to announce the "sign on the bus," the destination of the meeting: what you hope to achieve as the result of bringing these people together.

Background Information

To further improve meeting effectiveness, handing out background information on the subject well in advance gives everyone a chance to plan, prepare, get organized, and be ready to make the meeting as efficient as possible.

Only invite those whose presence is essential. Avoid the natural tendency to invite people to the meeting so that they do not feel left out. The kindest thing you can do as a meeting leader is to tell people that they do not need to attend this particular meeting. They can continue with whatever else they are doing and, if something comes up that is important, you will let them know about it later.

If you are a meeting participant, do everything possible to avoid attending the meeting if you don't need to be there. Ask the meeting leader if there is some other way that you can make whatever contribution is required of you.

If it is still important that you attend the meeting, ask the meeting leader to discuss the point or points that are relevant to you right at the beginning so that you can make your contribution and then politely excuse yourself.

Make Your Contribution Visual

If you are making a PowerPoint or a written presentation, be sure to have copies of your notes available to hand out with the agenda when you begin. Fully 70 percent of people are visual in the way that they absorb and comprehend information. Only 30 percent of people are verbal. This means that unless a visual person can see the information in writing or pictures, they do not process or retain it for any period of time. This is why it is an excellent idea for you to write down all the key points and make sure that each person has these key points in front of them as you go through them in the meeting.

Writing things out or creating visuals increases meeting efficiency. When people can see what it is you are talking about or discussing, they are much more capable of offering contributions and insights as the meeting progresses.

End Strongly

Every meeting should end with a clear agreement about the next actions. Who is going to do what, by what time, and to what standard? How and when will you or someone else follow up on the action commitments made in the meeting? What happens now?

Think of a meeting as a tool that is absolutely essential if you want to work through and with other people. Resolve to become excellent at using this tool to the best advantage of yourself and your organization. Become known as the kind of person who holds excellent meetings that other people enjoy attending and from which they benefit both personally and in their careers.

TWENTY-ONE

Meetings as Management in Action

MEETINGS ARE one of the single most important tools that you can use to advance your career. Your future as a manager, as a leader, and as an executive is going to be in direct proportion to your ability to conduct meetings well, and to conduct yourself well in meetings.

Become brilliant on the basics. Approach each meeting as if it was an important part of your future, because often it is.

Good Meeting Etiquette

First, plan in advance. Think through what type of meeting it is going to be, who needs to be in attendance at the meeting, and when they need to attend to discuss the items that are relevant to them.

Prepare a complete agenda. Invite the input of other people to the agenda. Practice the "no surprises" principle. People should come to the meeting with a good understanding of what is to be discussed and with sufficient background information to make a valuable contribution to the discussion.

Start and stop the meeting on time. Remember, because of the hourly income of each of the participants, meetings are an expensive investment of the company's money. Some meetings cost hundreds and even thousands of dollars of salary and wage time. Time spent in meetings must therefore not to be wasted.

Stay on Track

Keep the meeting on track. When people bring up another subject, say something like, "Why don't we take that subject off-line and discuss it after the meeting?"

Think in terms of action. A meeting that does not end in specific action commitments by specific people is merely a circular discussion that goes around and around, and will go around again. Reach an action conclusion on each point on the agenda. Make a decision to either do something, do nothing, or put it off to a subsequent meeting for a final decision. Conclude the point and move on.

Follow up each meeting with the key people who have made action commitments. Be sure that each person knows what is to be done, when it is to be done, and what the next step will be. Never assume.

Finally, make a decision to become excellent at conducting meetings and participating in meetings. Use this extremely important business tool to accomplish more and better results for your organization and for yourself.

Conclusion

YOU CAN turn ordinary meetings into high-payoff opportunities for yourself and your company. You can guide, direct, and build your subordinates in meetings. You can impress your superiors by the way you participate in a meeting or by the way that you lead a meeting. You can get work done in meetings that can be done in no other way. You can solve problems, make decisions, influence and persuade people, and control the flow of events.

By reading and rereading the ideas in this book, you can become absolutely excellent in one of the most important activities in business life.